# Once Upon A Time Bible Stories
## Little David's Adventures

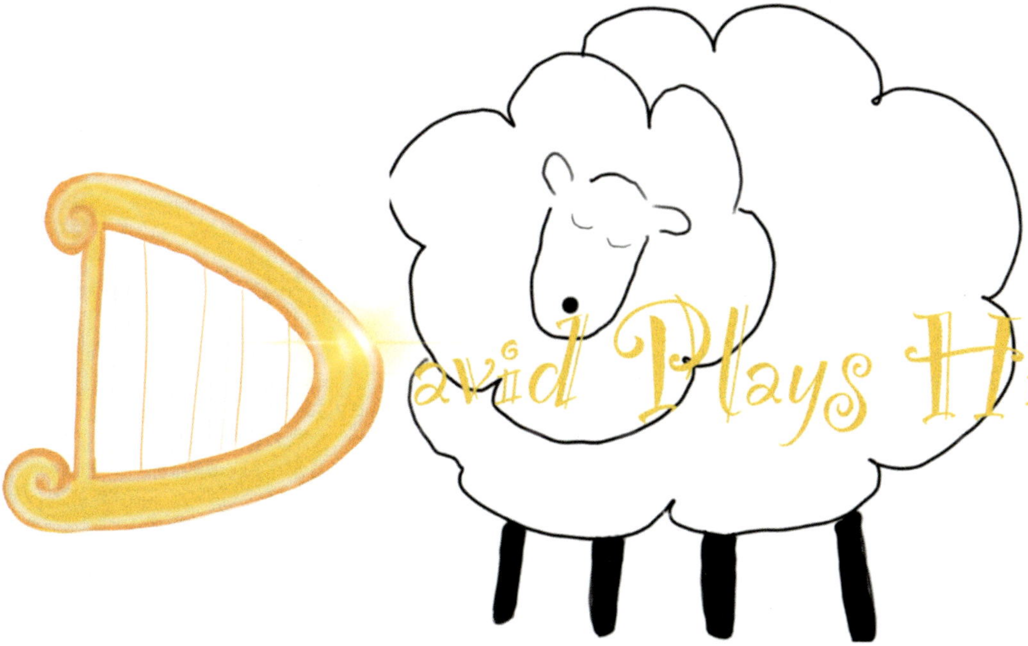

### David Plays His Harp

written by
Jody Reichelt

illustrated by
Jody Reichelt

# Once upon a time …

Little David is a shepherd.
He goes each day to tend his sheep.

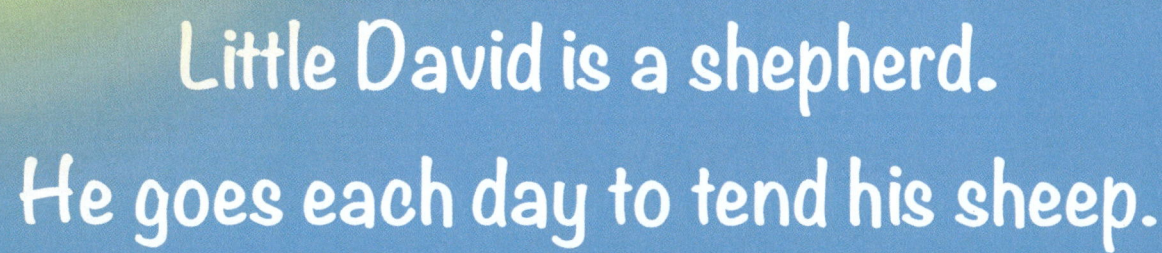

At night he plays his harp.

His harp puts the sheep to sleep.

# Saul is Israel's king.

He hears a sound that soothes his soul.

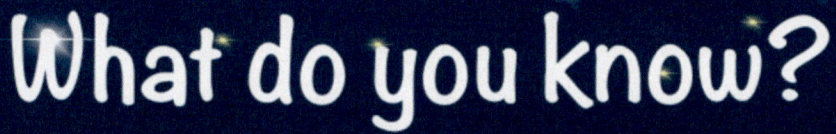

It's little David with his sheep.

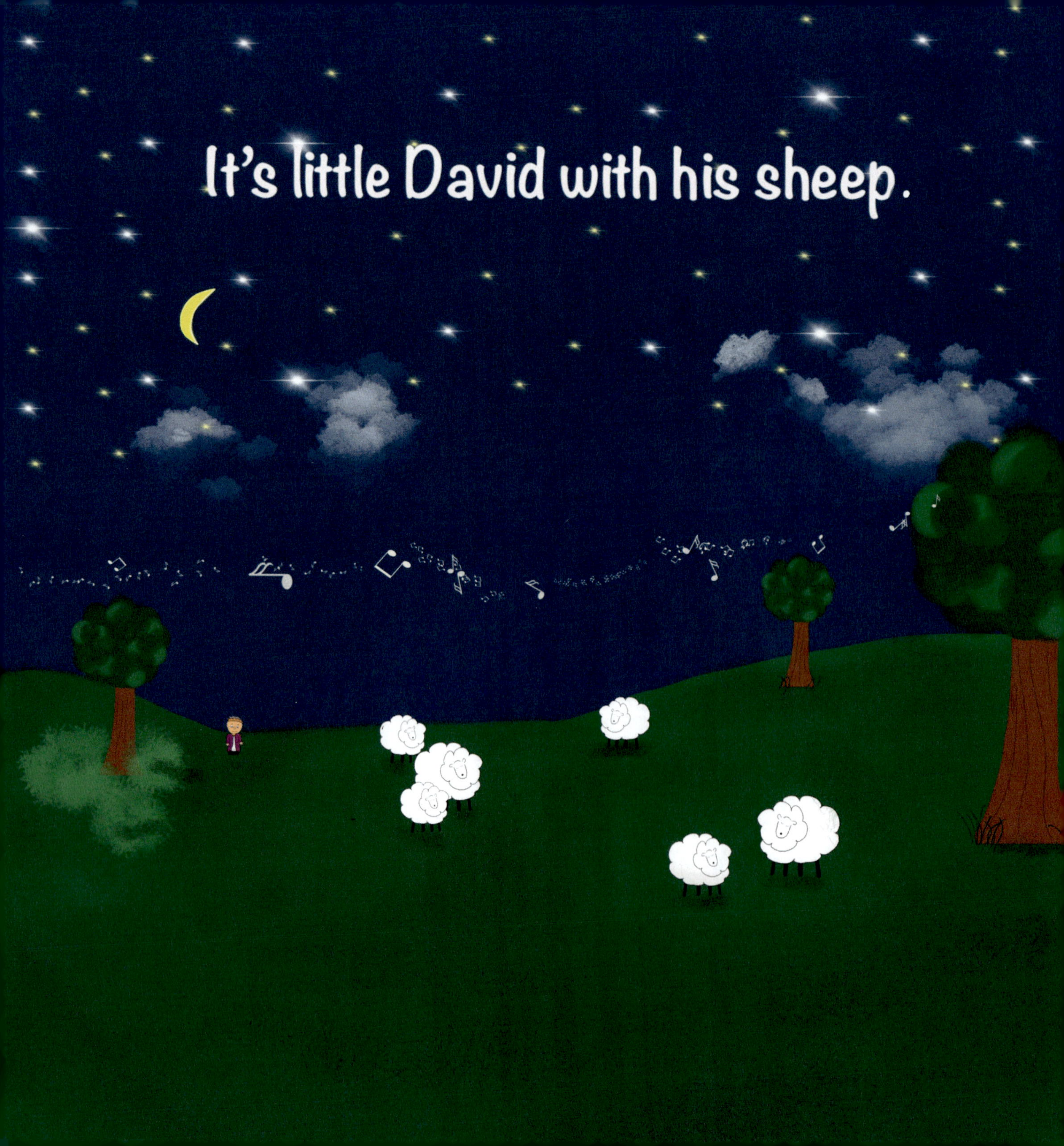

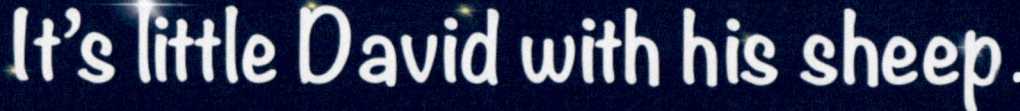

King Saul lays down to listen to the music.

He falls asleep with the sheep.

King Saul awakes in the morning.

He's so surprised! He found a way to shut his eyes and finally get some sleep!

# King Saul sends for little David!

Little David heads to the palace to play his harp that helps soothe the kings troubled heart.

every time Little David would play.

The end . . .

Till the next adventure . . .

# Once Upon A Time Bible Stories

## Little David's Adventures

David's Anointed King
David Plays His Harp
David Protects His Sheep

## Little David's Adventures
### Coloring Book Edition

David's Anointed King
David Plays His Harp
David Protects His Sheep

# Once Upon A Time Bible Stories

## Coming Soon
## Little Joseph's Adventures

Made in the USA
Las Vegas, NV
29 March 2025